GRIEVING THE LOSS

How to Survive When the World Around You Dies

DR. CANDICE E. COX, LCSW,CATP, CCTP

For permissions, inquiries, or speaking engagements, please contact:

KHAOS, Inc.
8790 Manchester Road, Suite 205A
St. Louis, MO 63144 www.khaosinc.org

Book Title: *Grieving the Loss: How to Survive When the World Around You Dies*

Author: Dr. Candice E. Cox, LCSW, CATP, CCTP
Cover Design by: Mercy Andrew
Interior Layout: Formatted by Mercy Andrew
Printed in the United States of America
First Edition: 2025
ISBN: 979-8-218-78341-9

This book is a work of nonfiction. Some names and identifying details have been changed to protect privacy. The author has drawn upon personal experiences, clinical insight, and trauma-informed practices to create this work. This book is not intended as a substitute for therapy, mental health treatment, or professional medical advice.

Dedication

To my kids, my momma, my granny, my Kima, Amy, the KHAOS team and Community.

You've all seen me through the storm. I appreciate each of you for the roles you've played in my life, whether it was wiping my tears, holding space for my silence, or reminding me of my strength when I forgot who I was.

To my ex-husband, thank you for our children, for the good times, because it wasn't all bad, for loving me the best you could, and for letting me go when it was time for us to grow in different directions

This book wouldn't exist without the pain and the journey from CHAOS to KHAOS, but more importantly, it wouldn't exist without the people who helped me turn that pain into a testimony of healing and growing. #mentalwellnessisdope #khaosmindset

Foreword

The first time I heard Candice say, *"Nobody teaches you how to grieve someone who is still alive,"* the room went quiet in that way truth makes a room go quiet. Shoulders softened. Breaths came deeper. People nodded before their minds could even form words. That is the power of Dr. Candice E. Cox, LCSW. She says the thing you have been living and cannot yet name, then she gives you language, tools, and a path back to yourself.

This book is that path.

Grieving the Loss: How to Survive When the World Around You Dies is a necessary guide for a kind of heartbreak our culture rarely acknowledges. We have rituals for funerals. We have casseroles and floral sprays and programs printed with dates. What we do not have are rituals for the losses that keep walking around, posting photos, sending sporadic texts, and showing up in our nervous systems at 2 a.m. We do not have casseroles for the silent deaths of trust, safety, belonging, and the identity we built inside a story that stopped being true. Candice has written the book that fills this aching gap.

I have watched Candice do this work in rooms and communities that hold both tenderness and storm. She brings clinical rigor and lived honesty in equal measure. As a therapist, she knows the research. As a woman, a mother, a daughter, a leader, she knows the cost. She does not posture. She does not perform. She tells the truth and then shows you how to hold it without burning yourself down.

What you hold in your hands is not "content." It is craft and care. Candice names the patterns that keep us tethered to pain, the trauma-bonding that masquerades as devotion, the toxic loyalty that erodes dignity, the bargains we strike with our own souls in the name of keeping a family, a friendship, a partnership, an image intact. She does not stop at naming. She equips.

The KHAOS Mindset is not a slogan. It is a practical psychology of change. RAW helps you Realize, Admit, and Work through the truth you have been circling. RESET trains your mind and body to Remember Every Situation Encourages Thought so you interrupt survival loops and rebuild with intention. FREE invites you to Forgive, Release, Embrace, and Elevate so you do not just leave what harmed you, you outgrow it. PATIENT gives you a breath-by-breath protocol when grief surges and language disappears: Pause And Think. Inhale. Exhale. Now Talk or Tap Out. The order matters. Your breathing matters. You matter.

Candice writes with open hands. She offers clinical insight where it serves, then anchors each insight in story. She does not pathologize your responses to harm. She normalizes them and then shows you how to transform them. You will see yourself in these pages — not in a way that shames, but in a way that dignifies.

If you have ever felt like a ghost in your own life, if you have smiled in public and unraveled in private, if you have been both the dependable one and the disappearing one, this book will meet you where you are and walk with you toward where you want to go.

For the parents holding it together for children who are grieving what they cannot name, there is language here. For the partners who stayed too long because familiar pain felt safer than unfamiliar peace, there is a mirror here that does not judge. For the leaders, the healers, the helpers who pour from empty cups and call it strength, there is permission here to stop surviving your own life and start living it.

One of my favorite qualities in Candice's work is her integrity with complexity. She will not sell you a fairy tale of instant freedom. She will not ask you to bypass sadness or silence anger. She will invite you to feel every feeling without letting any single feeling take the wheel. She will ask you to grieve what never became, to accept what is, to honor what was, and to choose what is next with clarity. She will remind you that acceptance is not an endorsement of harm. Acceptance is a reclamation of your power to decide.

If you are reading this at the kitchen table after the kids are asleep, if you are in a parking lot gathering yourself before you go inside, if you are in a therapist's waiting room, if you are between text messages you know you should not answer, let me say this clearly: you are not broken. You are not behind. You are not hard to love. You are human in a season that asks more of your heart than you learned to carry. This book will show you how to share the load with breath, with language, with practice, with community, with time.

Here is how to use what Candice gives you: Read slowly. Dog-ear the pages that hold you. Work the questions at the end of each chapter with a pen that will not smudge because tears will come and that is all right. Try the skills often so they are available when you are not. Teach them to your children in small ways. Breathe with them. Name feelings in your home. Write letters you may never send. Set boundaries that keep your peace safe. Ask for help. Rest when your body asks. Celebrate tiny repairs. Keep going.

I have known many brilliant clinicians and many courageous storytellers. Candice is rare because she is both at once. She brings scholarship to her tenderness and tenderness to her scholarship. She brings her whole self. That is why these pages carry weight. They have lived. They have been tested. They have been refined in therapy rooms, hospital corridors, school offices, sanctuaries, and kitchens where truth finally had a seat at the table.

If you let it, this book will not simply inform you. It will change your relationship with yourself. It will raise the standard for how you allow others to love you. It will help you tell the truth in sentences you can live. It will teach you to stand up different. Not tougher. Truer.

Grief will come. It will come in the form of endings you choose and endings that choose you. It will come in the form of people who cannot be who you needed them to be. It will come in the form of versions of you that protected you once and are now asking to retire. When it comes, reach for these pages. Let the KHAOS tools live on your nightstand and in your notes app. Let them live in your breath. You can survive when the world around you dies. You can do more than survive. You can become.

With respect and warmth, I offer this foreword with my full heart. As a thought leader in the coaching industry, I can tell you this book does what few works dare to do. It doesn't just inform, it transforms. It shifts how we think about grief, how we speak about healing, and how we teach others to reclaim themselves after loss.

Dr. Candice Cox has given us a body of work that belongs not only on bookshelves but in living rooms, therapy rooms, and sacred spaces where real healing happens.

To every reader, welcome. You are in capable hands. Take a breath. Begin.

--- Sophia Casey, MCC
Master Certified Executive Coach & CEO, ICLI RISING
ICF-accredited coach training & leadership development institute
iclirising.com

A letter to my babies

Dear Jai and Cam,

My heart in human form, my why, my reasons for getting up when life tried to sit me down...

This book is as much yours as it is mine.

You have watched me unravel, rebuild, break again, and bloom. You've seen tears that weren't yours fall during conversations, felt tension you didn't cause fill the room, and heard apologies I never wanted to say out loud. You've lived in the quiet of the chaos, right beside me, as I tried to figure out how to mother while mourning.

I wrote this book because I never want you to think that pain means you have to stay stuck. I never want you to believe that love should cost you *you*. I never want you to confuse survival with wholeness. You deserve joy, peace, rest, and people who choose you fully, just like I had to learn to choose myself.

Every chapter, every paragraph, every tear-stained sentence is a step toward healing not just for me, but for you, too. For us.

You are not the reason our family changed. You are the reason I refused to stay broken. Watching you grow into beautiful, thoughtful, emotionally intelligent humans makes me proud beyond words. I know this journey hasn't been easy. I know the grief hit you, too, even if you didn't always have the words to say it.

But look at us now.

Still standing. Still healing. Still together.

I love you more than you'll ever know.

With all the love in the world from my heart to yours,

~Momma aka Candi, the biggest C not the little one 😊

Table of Contents

PART I: THE ROOT

How to Use This Book

This isn't just a book to read, it's a book to *work through*. You can read my story from beginning to end like a memoir, or you can treat it like a healing toolkit, pausing wherever the KHAOS Check-Ins and journal prompts hit you.

Every time you see **✍ Reflect. Release. Rebuild.**, I'm inviting you to stop, breathe, and face your truth, not the pretty version you post online, but the raw, unfiltered truth that needs your attention.

The KHAOS Mindset tools — RAW, RESET, PATIENT, FREE are here to guide you. You'll see them woven into my story, but they're also here for *your* story. Take notes in the margins. Answer the prompts. Cry, write, rip out pages if you need to (but hold on to them in case you need them later).

This book is yours now. Let it be messy. Healing always is.

Introduction
When the World Ends and You're Still Breathing

This is not just a story about divorce. It's a story about grieving the loss of someone who is still alive… and finding yourself in the wreckage.

He said he wanted to take time to "grow."

Said the space would be good for both of us.

Said maybe we could come back together stronger after a year.

Lies.

What he really wanted was to do his own thing without feeling guilty.

He wanted freedom without accountability and access without commitment.

He wanted to explore a new life, keep me on the shelf, and call it "growth."

And me? I was still trying.

Still believing.

Still loving a version of him that no longer existed.

I'll never forget the day he stood in the bathroom while I was in the tub. I was just minding my business, sitting, soaking, listening to India Arie with no clue my life was about to blow up.

He asked me, "Are you happy?"

I told him no.

"Are you unhappy?"

Again, I said no.

He looked confused and said, "So… what are you?"

I answered, "I'm just here."

What I didn't know in that moment was that the newest affair had already started.

He had already chosen her emotionally, physically, and mentally.

And he was trying to keep both lives alive.

I wasn't happy. I wasn't unhappy. I was numb.

The kind of numb that only comes after years of giving everything to someone who couldn't see you, hear you, or hold you down.

The kind of numb that signals the death of something sacred, even though the body hasn't dropped yet.

That conversation wasn't the beginning of my grief.

I had been carrying **anticipatory grief** for quite a while.

But it was the moment I realized what had been dying was finally about to end.

Even after the divorce was filed, we tried counseling.

We fought through emotions, co-parenting, confusion, and pain.

But he was still in the affair.

Still telling us both different stories.

Still living two lives.

And I was stuck in the middle of a slow, silent emotional funeral.

When the papers were signed, the house was clear, and me and the kids were settling into our new normal, I flatlined.

But this book isn't just about **my story.**

It's about **yours** too, the one you may not have told anyone yet.

This is for the woman who's had to keep parenting through pain.

Who's gone to work with a broken heart.

Who's smiled through family functions, school events, and holidays while silently screaming on the inside.

Who's explaining to her kids why the family fell apart… while never really getting the answers herself.

This is for the ones who stayed too long.

The ones who left too late.

The ones who are just now starting to find themselves again.

And this isn't only for people going through divorce.

This is for anyone grieving the loss of a relationship, **romantic, platonic, or familial,** with someone who is still alive.

A best friend who betrayed you.

A parent who never showed up.

A sibling you had to walk away from.

A partner who disappeared emotionally before they ever left physically.

Grieving someone who is still breathing is a special kind of pain.

You lose the connection, the safety, the identity you built around them but not the presence.

You still see them. Still hear about them. Still have to figure out how to exist without the role they once played in your life.

That's the grief this book holds space for.

And that's where the **KHAOS Mindset** comes in.

I created KHAOS, Keep Healing And Overcoming Struggles, a framework to help individuals learn how to assess, address, and reduce the impact of toxic and traumatic stress before the divorce.

But I leaned on it like oxygen throughout the healing process.

It became my compass when I couldn't find solid ground.

This mindset helped me peel back the layers.

Sit in the mess.

Name the grief.

And do the work to come out on the other side.

The tools inside it saved me, and now I'm sharing them with you.

The KHAOS Tools You'll Learn:

💜 **RAW**: Realize, Admit, Work through.

Start by getting honest about the pain, the patterns, and your part in the story.

💜 **RESET:** Remember Every Situation Encourages Thought.

When your thoughts spiral and emotions flood, RESET helps you pause, reflect, and reframe.

💜 **PATIENT:** Pause And Think, Inhale/Exhale, Now Talk or Tap Out.

This tool helps you respond instead of react, especially in moments when you want to blow up or break down.

❤️ **FREE**: Forgive, Release, Embrace, Elevate.

Because real healing isn't about forgetting. It's about freeing yourself from the grip of what hurt you.

You'll see these tools woven throughout the book along with journal prompts and check-ins to help you process your pain.

Because this isn't just a book.

It's a healing experience.

It's a mirror, a map, and a hand to hold while you find your way forward.

If you're here, I want you to breathe.

Inhale what you've become.

Exhale what you had to let go of to get here.

The grief may have knocked the wind out of you, but it didn't take your power.

You're still here.

And that means your healing has already begun.

Let's do the work. Together.

You don't need to be perfect to start, just willing.

Willing to feel.

Willing to be honest.

Willing to heal.

And I promise:

There's freedom on the other side of this grief.

Let's grieve. Let's grow. Let's break FREE.

With love and compassion,

Candice

The Science Behind the Struggle: Anger is often a protective response to betrayal or abandonment and can mask deeper emotions like grief, fear, or shame. (American Psychological Association)

Chapter 1

Living Ghosts

"I had to grieve the man I married, even though he was still breathing."

You ever grieve someone who's still alive?

That shit hits different.

No funeral. No obituary. No flowers. Just silence. Just shock. Just a version of you that no longer exists and a version of them you never imagined.

I call them **living ghosts**, people who are no longer in your life emotionally, spiritually, mentally, or safely... but they're still walking around. And sometimes? They're still showing up to birthday parties, still co-parenting, still popping up in your dreams, your inbox, or your triggers.

For me, grieving the loss of my marriage was like watching my world burn from the inside out. On paper, we were together. In real life? I was doing everything alone. Raising the kids, running the businesses, managing the house, and the man I called "husband" was a stranger playing video games in the basement.

The kids started calling him "Daddy in the basement."

That's how far we had drifted. He came upstairs to eat, sleep, and request sex. Not much else.

I didn't want to accept it at first. I held on to the fantasy that we could make it work. But slowly, I realized: I wasn't grieving a breakup. I was grieving who I thought he was. Who I needed him to be. Who I lied to myself about him being.

And that hurt worse than any goodbye.

The Pattern Beneath the Pain

When I finally sat still, I started to notice the pattern.

I had married both my mother and my father in one man.

The inconsistency, the pain, the manipulation, the absence.

It was all familiar.

Familiar... not healthy.

And that's the trap. You think because it feels familiar, it must be love. But sometimes, what feels familiar is just a repeat of your trauma.

My mama taught me love was inconsistent. That love shows up when you do what's right and hurts you when you don't.

My daddy taught me love disappears. That love lies. That love shows up with gifts and empty apologies and always needs fixing.

TV told me if I just held on long enough, fought hard enough, sacrificed enough, I'd get my happily ever after.

But life? Life showed me the truth: I was loving from a place of brokenness. I was building castles in sand. And when the water rose, it all washed away.

Emotional Casualties & The Lies We Live

After the separation, inboxes from random women started rolling in.

At least seven different women confirmed what I suspected all along:

I was in an open marriage but didn't have a clue.

And I'll be honest, getting an STD test after 17 years of being faithful and married?

Humiliating. I felt dirty. Violated. Betrayed. That's the kind of grief you can't prepare for. It doesn't come with a playbook. It comes with shame, silence, and the feeling that you were stupid for not seeing it sooner.

But I wasn't stupid. I was committed. I was loyal. I was loving someone from the deepest parts of me, the kind of love that sees potential even when the reality is painful.

And still... I didn't hate him. To this day, I don't. Because somewhere in there, I realized the truth that cracked me wide open:

He didn't know how to love me.

Not in a healthy way.

Not in a way that honored me, protected me, or made me feel safe.

And I didn't know how to require that kind of love.

I didn't know how to ask for more because I was still healing from the parts of me that believed I didn't deserve more.

That's the part people don't talk about. We focus on what they did, but we rarely sit with what we allowed. The ways we ignored red flags. The way we downplayed our needs.

The way we over-explained, over-accommodated, and over-functioned... just to keep the peace.

Those are the emotional casualties. The parts of you that die while you're still in the relationship. The boundaries you abandon. The silence you swallow.

The identity you bury under their needs, moods, and egos.

And then, when it all falls apart, you're left grieving not just the person...

But the version of yourself you lost trying to keep them.

That's where the real grief lives. In the quiet compromises.

In the lonely moments spent sleeping next to someone who no longer saw you.

In the realization that you built a life with someone who wasn't even emotionally present in it.

So no, I don't hate him. But I had to stop betraying myself for the sake of calling it love. Because love without truth isn't love. Love without safety isn't love.

Love without healing is just codependency wrapped in emotional chaos.

RAW Truth

In KHAOS, we get **RAW** with ourselves.

We:

- **Realize** the truth about our patterns
- **Admit** how we've been impacted and how we've contributed
- **Work** to create a new normal

And my truth was: I was in a trauma bond.

One that I had mistaken for unconditional love.

But unconditional love should never require you to disappear in order for someone else to stay.

I had to make a decision: stay in the familiar pain, or risk the unknown for the sake of healing.

Healing Through the Hurt

There were days I couldn't breathe.

Days I begged God to take the pain away.

Days I cried in silence and smiled for the kids.

Being a mother while grieving is one of the hardest things I've ever done.

But in the rubble, I found pieces of me.

Pieces I had lost trying to be everything for everyone.

Pieces I'd buried just to survive.

This chapter, this grief, this pain, it taught me that you can survive the death of a relationship… even when no one died. But the only way out is through.

So if you're grieving someone still living, whether it's a parent, partner, or version of yourself, I want you to know:

You're not alone.

You're not crazy.

And this is your permission to mourn what never became, to bury the fairy tale, and to finally make peace with your truth.

KHAOS Check-In – After Chapter Reflection

- Who are the living ghosts you're still holding on to?
- What lies have you told yourself about your relationship?
- What did your mother/father/childhood teach you about love?
- How are you coping, surviving or healing?
- What version of you are you ready to unearth again?

Chapter 2

Love, Lessons, and Lies

"I didn't know how to love healthy, because I never saw it done."

Getting to the root of why you choose who you choose is not for the weak.

It starts off innocent, just asking questions.

"Why do I keep picking people who hurt me?"

"Why do I stay even when I'm unhappy?"

"Why do I feel like I have to earn love?"

And then boom, you're face to face with the patterns. The generational curses. The wounds you inherited. You realize you didn't just pick these people by accident... you were trained for them.

Nobody pulled you aside and said, "Hey, let me teach you how to love someone who neglects you, cheats on you, lies to your face, and makes you question your worth." But life did. Your environment did. Your childhood did.

So you end up loving people who reflect what's *familiar*, not what's *healthy*.

The Blueprint You Didn't Know You Had

My mama didn't sit me down and say "love is inconsistent and conditional," but she showed me.

She showed me with her silence, her outbursts, her punishments that came from fear instead of love.

I learned early that love could be snatched away if you made someone upset. That love had rules.

That love was earned by performing.

My daddy taught me another lesson, how to love a ghost.

He was there… but not really. He'd pop in and out.

He told me what I wanted to hear, but never showed me what I needed to see.

His love taught me to accept lies, to ignore my gut, to let charm override consistency.

And then came TV. That damn fairy tale version of love.

The "ride or die," "struggle together," "fight until the end" love.

Nobody told me real love don't require a war just to stay afloat.

So I took those lessons and stitched them together.

That was my love blueprint.

I Married My Parents… and Didn't Even Know It

It hit me like a brick one day.

I looked at my life and realized:

I married the worst parts of both my parents.

The inconsistency, the emotional neglect, the dishonesty, the absence… it was all there.

And the craziest part? I tolerated it.

I justified it.

Because it felt normal.

Because it felt like home.

And that's the scariest part of all—how you can normalize dysfunction so deeply that you don't even realize you're sleeping next to your trauma every night.

You think you're building a life.

But you're just reliving an old wound.

Love vs. Trauma Bond

Let's be clear:

What I had was broken version of love.

It was a trauma bond dressed in a wedding ring and displayed as family.

It was that familiar ache.

That pull toward the person who reminds you of the pain you never healed from.

See, trauma bonds aren't built on love; they're built on survival.

The highs and lows. The making up just to break up.

The "maybe this time it'll be different" that keeps you locked in.

You convince yourself it's love because you feel something.

But feeling "something" isn't the same as being loved safely.

The Science Behind the Struggle: *Depression and grief often coexist. Prolonged stress can dysregulate the hypothalamic-pituitary-adrenal (HPA) axis, impacting mood and energy. (National Institute of Mental Health)*

The Lies We Tell Ourselves

We don't just get lied to; we lie to ourselves.

"I can fix this."

"It's not that bad."

"They didn't mean it."

"I just need to be more patient."

"We just need to get back to how we used to be."

You rewrite the truth over and over to fit the version of the relationship you want, instead of facing the version that actually exists.

That's how we stay stuck.

That's how we stay hurt.

Breaking the Pattern Means Unlearning the Lie

Healing starts when you stop lying to yourself.

When you stop blaming everyone else and start asking yourself what made you available to that kind of love in the first place.

And that's not about shame, it's about **awareness.**

You can't change what you don't acknowledge.

And you can't heal what you keep pretending doesn't hurt.

The hardest truth I had to face?

I never learned how to love.

And I damn sure never learned how to be loved right.

So I had to go back to the root.

To the little girl who was trying to be enough for people who never knew how to show up.

To the teenager who didn't feel safe expressing her emotions.

To the grown woman who kept choosing pain in hopes that it would eventually turn into peace.

I had to go back and rescue her.

KHAOS Check-In: Love, Lessons & Lies

- What did your parents teach you about love, directly or indirectly?
- Where did you learn how to love? Who modeled it for you?
- What patterns in your relationships keep repeating?
- When have you confused familiarity with love?
- What lies are you still telling yourself to justify staying connected to someone who hurts you?

RAW Reflection:

You didn't deserve what happened to you.

But you do deserve to heal from it.

And healing means you stop blaming them… and start choosing you.

This is where you start learning a new way to love, one that starts with you.

Chapter 3

Toxic Loyalty & Emotional Casualties

"Just because someone holds a title in your life doesn't mean they deserve a role in your future."

There's a kind of loyalty that looks like love on the outside... but feels like death on the inside.

The kind that has you suffering in silence, staying out of obligation, or breaking your own boundaries just to avoid making somebody else uncomfortable. That's not love. That's not strength. That's toxic loyalty.

Let's talk about it.

Toxic Loyalty: When Pain Wears a Mask

Toxic loyalty is being loyal to someone just because of the role they play in your life, even when their actions hurt you.

We do it with parents, partners, pastors, and play cousins.

We do it because we were trained that family is family, no matter what.

We do it because we were taught that loyalty is everything... even if it costs you your peace, your sanity, your identity.

You ever stay connected to someone not because they bring you joy, but because you feel guilty walking away?

You ever find yourself constantly explaining their behavior to other people?

You ever have to remind yourself why you love someone... because deep down you're starting to forget?

That's the impact of toxic loyalty.

It makes you shrink.

It makes you question yourself.

It makes you bleed emotionally in places nobody can see.

The Emotional Casualties of Staying Too Long

People talk about trauma like it only lives in the big, loud, explosive moments. But most of the damage? It happens in the quiet. The subtle. The repeated. The familiar.

That's where **emotional casualties** live.

Emotional casualties are the losses you carry that nobody talks about:

- The respect you lost for your partner after the tenth lie.
- The trust you lost in your parent after the betrayal.
- The voice you lost from not speaking up.

- The joy that got buried under pretending everything was okay.

It's not always one big wound. Sometimes it's a thousand tiny cuts.

And the longer you stay… the more pieces of yourself you lose.

Until one day you look up and realize: **You don't recognize yourself anymore.**

My Breaking Point: The Loss Behind the Loyalty

I stayed for a long time.

Longer than I should've.

Not because I didn't see the truth… but because I didn't want to admit it.

I didn't want to be another failed marriage statistic.

I didn't want my kids to grow up in a "broken" home.

I didn't want to believe that I had invested all this time, all this energy, all this love… just to be left with pieces.

But here's the truth:

I wasn't staying for love.

I was staying because I felt responsible.

Responsible for his healing.

Responsible for keeping the family together.

Responsible for proving everyone wrong.

And while I was busy being loyal to everyone else… I was abandoning **me.**

When Loyalty Becomes a Cage

We talk a lot about betrayal.

But we rarely talk about the betrayal of self.

You ever betray your own needs just to keep the peace?

You ever silence your voice so someone else can feel more powerful?

You ever downplay your pain just to keep the image of the relationship intact?

That's what toxic loyalty does. It trains you to survive, not thrive.

It tells you:

"Don't rock the boat."

"Be the bigger person."

"Stick it out no matter what."

And you do. Until one day, you wake up and you're drowning.

The Science Behind the Struggle: *Bargaining is a common grief stage where individuals try to regain control or reverse pain, often by minimizing their own needs. (Kübler-Ross Grief Model)*

The KHAOS Shift: Breaking Free From What's Breaking You

In KHAOS, we learn that healing ain't about proving loyalty to people who benefit from your silence.

It's about getting **RAW** with the truth and RESETTING your story.

Because the truth is:

- You can love someone and still need to let them go.
- You can forgive someone and still protect your peace.
- You can honor the past without being held hostage by it.

I had to get clear on the difference between loyalty and self-sacrifice.

I had to stop confusing pain with purpose.

I had to unlearn that love meant suffering.

That meant asking myself:

- "Why do I keep people around who drain me?"
- "What am I so afraid of losing?"

- "When did I start believing that I didn't deserve more?"

Because **healing begins at the root.**

And for me, the root was in how I was taught to love, endure, and stay... even when it was killing me softly.

KHAOS Check-In: Unpacking Toxic Loyalty

- Who are you being loyal to out of guilt, not love?
- What parts of yourself have you lost by staying too long?
- What emotional casualties have you collected over time?
- Are you protecting the relationship... or protecting your wound?
- What would it mean to choose you?

RAW Reflection:

It's not disloyal to walk away from people who refuse to grow.

It's not selfish to want peace.

It's survival. It's healing. It's you reclaiming your power.

Letting go of toxic loyalty is not betrayal. Think about it, you know what it feels like to hurt and hold on, you deserve to know what it feels like to heal and move forward. At this point it's about finding yourself on the other side. **You owe that to you. Understand, some relationships may have to end or change** because you don't like who you have to be to maintain them and that's ok. Somebody has to choose you let it be you.

PART II: THE STORM

Chapter 4

Anger "Here I Am, Thinking You Were for Me…"

"The most painful part about betrayal is realizing the person who hurt you is the one you loved the most."

Anger is loud.

It shows up in your chest like fire.

It sits behind your eyes, waiting to flood out as tears.

It builds in your body when you've held in too much for too long.

And when you're grieving someone who's still alive, especially someone you loved?

Anger shows up often and unapologetically.

It's not always rage. Sometimes it's sarcasm. Sometimes it's that deep silence that says "if I open my mouth, I might burn all this shit down."

The Inbox That Broke Me

After the divorce was filed, I started getting messages.

Not from friends. Not from supporters. From **women.**

Women I'd never met. Women who had stories. Receipts. Screenshots.

Over the course of 17 years, the man I built my life with cheated on me at least 7 times. And that's just what I know about. I'm sure there's more. There's always more.

And in the middle of all this betrayal, I found myself at the doctor's office, getting a full STD panel. Seventeen years of faithfulness, and here I was, scared of what I might've been exposed to. Scared that I was being punished for his lies.

I sat in that cold room, paper gown and all, feeling humiliated.

Not just violated, but discarded. Like, I was never even considered. Pissed because he played Russian roulette with my life and took my choice away.

I felt dirty. Ashamed. Furious.

When Love Feels Like Disrespect

See, anger doesn't just show up because of what happened.

Anger shows up when your trust gets stomped on.

When your sacrifices get ignored.

When the person you were loyal to disrespects the very foundation you built your life on.

I gave him everything.

And in return, I got gaslighted. Lied to. Embarrassed.

I kept showing up, giving the best of me to someone who didn't even value me.

And you know what hurts worse than betrayal?

Realizing how long you stayed after the first lie.

The Journal Entry That Let Me Breathe

One day, I sat down and wrote it out. No filter. No sugar. Just the truth:

"Here I am, thinking you were for me... and you were for everybody. Damn."

You embarrassed me.

You violated me.

You pushed me.

You cursed me.

You lied to me.

You cheated on me.

And still... I loved you. I didn't hate you. I loved you so hard it hurt.

But I had to realize—loving you didn't mean losing me.

I had to choose me, even though I loved you.

You can't love me right because you're not right. And I had to stop thinking that if I loved you enough, you'd change. You didn't.

And maybe... you couldn't.

That journal entry saved me from exploding.

Because when we don't express anger safely, we turn it inward.

We start blaming ourselves.

We start questioning our worth.

We start calling what we endured "normal."

The Layers of My Rage

There are levels to this.

I was angry at him for the lies, the infidelity, the gaslighting.

But I was also angry at **myself.**

For staying.

For making excuses.

For thinking I was the exception.

For praying over a relationship that was breaking me instead of blessing me.

That's the part that nobody tells you about, the part where you won't just be mad at them. You'll be mad at yourself. And that rage? That rage cuts deep.

KHAOS and the Power of Naming It

In KHAOS, we don't silence our anger.

We honor it.

We name it.

We explore what it's protecting.

Because anger is always a bodyguard.

It shows up when pain is too heavy to hold alone.

Anger isn't the enemy. Suppressing it is.

So I had to stop bottling it up. I had to get RAW.

- **Realize** the pain I buried under loyalty
- **Admit** how long I betrayed myself to keep the peace
- **Work** to express what I felt without burning myself down in the process

The Science Behind the Struggle: *Denial is a trauma response. The brain sometimes suppresses truth to protect the body from emotional overwhelm. (Van der Kolk, *The Body Keeps the Score*)*

The Autopilot That Almost Took Me Out

When I really stepped back, I realized something terrifying:

We were both operating on autopilot.

He checked out emotionally.

I shut down.

We lived in the same house, different worlds.

Barely talking. No affection. No connection.

He coped by running to women, smoking weed, drinking alcohol, and other distractions.

I coped by burying myself in work, the kids, responsibility. I was frozen and he was in full flight mode.

We were strangers, roommates with kids. Nothing left between us but shared bills and broken dreams.

So when people say, "I can't believe y'all divorced," I say, "I can't believe we lasted that long."

From Rage to Realization

Eventually, the anger turned into clarity.

I realized I wasn't just mad at what he did.

I was mad because I gave him a role in my life that he was never qualified to hold.

He didn't break my heart.

I broke it by handing it to someone who didn't know how to carry it.

That doesn't excuse his actions.

But it gave me back my power.

Because accountability is not about blame, it's about ownership. And I had to own the role I played in my own pain. At the end of the day I had to be real with myself, I married potential and divorced reality. It hurt to come to that conclusion but I couldn't move forward without being honest with me. Cognitive dissonance is real and I was never going to have the life I wanted, needed, and desired staying in the marriage I was in.

KHAOS Check-In: Sitting with the Rage

- Who are you angry with, and why?
- What does your anger want you to know?
- Have you created space to express your rage safely?
- What role did you play in holding on to someone who kept hurting you?
- What boundaries did you ignore in the name of "love"?

RAW Reflection:

Your anger is not weakness.

It's wisdom. It's warning. It's wake-up.

Let it speak. Let it breathe.

Then let it guide you to the truth you've been avoiding.

Because you can't heal what you keep excusing.

And you can't rebuild while holding on to the ashes.

Chapter 5

Sadness "Daddy in the basement"

"I was married, but I felt like a single woman, alone in every way that mattered."

There's a sadness that sits on your chest so heavy, it feels like you're breathing through bricks.

You wake up with it.

Go to sleep with it.

Carry it into the kitchen, into the car, into the workplace, into the bathroom where you cry in silence so nobody sees.

It's not just heartbreak.

It's exhaustion.

Emotional, mental, spiritual exhaustion from trying to make something work that's been broken for a long time.

Married and Still Alone

There was a point in my marriage where I realized I was doing it all.

Cooking.

Raising the kids.

Running the businesses.

Paying the bills.

Protecting the image.

Covering for his absence.

Carrying the weight of both of us on my shoulders.

And yet... I was married.

To a man who was present in body but absent in spirit.

We lived in the same house, but I was alone in every way that counted.

That kind of loneliness hits different.

It doesn't just hurt. It hollows you.

I remember saying during one of our many conversations while we were separating, "I've loved you with every part of me and now I have nothing else to give." It wasn't said in anger, it was the cry of a woman who had been wrung out, who had poured from a cup that was now shattered. I had built, carried, prayed, begged, and sacrificed, but I couldn't breathe life into someone who had chosen to stop showing up.

And the hardest part? You start questioning yourself.

Is it me? Am I not enough?

You begin to shrink. Your laughter fades. Your light dims.

You become a shadow of who you were before the weight of loneliness started living in your home.

Two Houses, One Roof

There was this stretch of time where it felt like we were living in two different houses under the same roof. He didn't live in the basement, but it sure felt like he did. The basement was his escape, his man cave, his hiding place from the reality of being a husband, father, and partner. He'd come upstairs to eat, to sleep, to ask for intimacy, maybe watch a show, but rarely to connect.

It wasn't always like that. But over time, as life got heavy and our communication broke down, he just... disappeared. The kids stopped asking for him. They came to me for everything: homework, meals, emotional support, even their little victories. I became the default parent, while he became a shadow in the house.

Looking back now, I see that isolation for what it was an unspoken cry for help, mixed with his own unresolved pain and depression. But at the time? It felt like rejection. It felt like I was doing everything while carrying this giant, invisible weight. That kind of imbalance chips away at your spirit. I didn't just feel lonely, I felt unseen, unwanted, and unchosen in my own marriage.

Depression in Disguise

As a therapist, it's hard to know what's going on, have the tools to fix it, but feel helpless because you can't heal for someone else. And when you're stuck in the cycle, you can't even heal yourself.

I knew he was depressed. He barely came upstairs. He smoked. He drank. He isolated. He disconnected.

But you know what? I was depressed too.

There were so many times I spoke about the changes in behavior, discussed seeing someone, taking medication, doing something to address it. I couldn't make him. I was met with more distance, more isolation, more broken promises. We both sank deeper and deeper.

The difference? I didn't have the luxury of breaking down.

I was too busy keeping everything afloat — kids, work, home, stability — to even acknowledge my own decline. So I did what I had always done… I shut down.

Emotionally froze.

Went numb.

Survived.

Living on Empty

There's a silent pain that comes from having to be the strong one, especially when nobody is strong for you. I can't even count the number of times I cried in my car after holding it together all day. I would drive around the block just to release tears so I wouldn't look like what I was feeling when I got to the kids. People saw the degrees, the businesses, the polished exterior, but they didn't see the woman breaking behind closed doors.

I became so used to functioning in survival mode that I forgot what living felt like. I didn't realize how deep the numbness went until I looked in the mirror one day and couldn't recognize the woman staring back at me. I looked at my eyes and they looked so sad. I couldn't remember when they didn't look like that. In that moment I realized I missed the joyful me, the creative me, the me who could breathe without feeling crushed under responsibility and disappointment.

"Daddy in the Basement" Wasn't a Joke

We used to laugh about the kids calling him "Daddy in the basement." We would say it like it was some inside joke, like it was just a quirky part of our family dynamic. But looking back now, that was grief wrapped in humor. That was me trying to normalize the distance, pretending it was fine because I didn't want to face what it really meant.

The man I built a life with was disappearing before my eyes. Not just physically, but emotionally, mentally, and spiritually. It wasn't just about him being downstairs, it was about him not being here. Present. Engaged. Choosing us.

And while he hid in the basement, I hid behind performance. I became the smiling mom, the busy boss, the go-to friend. I was "fine" because I had no choice but to be fine. Nobody knew I was breaking, because I learned how to perfect the mask. I learned how to show up for everyone else while quietly crumbling inside.

The Mask of Overfunctioning

People assume depression always looks like sadness, like tears on a pillow or someone who can't get out of bed. But mine looked like overfunctioning. Hyper-independence. The "I got it" attitude that came with being let down too many times. My depression looked like running businesses, helping the kids with homework, and still showing up for speaking engagements while secretly drowning.

There were days I wanted to scream into a pillow until my throat gave out. Days I wanted to sleep through the entire year just to escape the heaviness of my reality. But instead, I smiled. I cooked dinner. I showed up to meetings. I played the part. Because if I stopped moving, the dam would break, and I didn't think I'd survive the flood.

Breaking Behind Closed Doors

My real breakdowns didn't happen in front of anyone. They happened in parking lots after long days. In the shower when the kids were asleep. In the tub when I could finally be alone with my thoughts. I'd sit in silence, tears rolling down my face, whispering prayers that felt like desperate pleas: "God, I'm trying. I'm holding on. But what now? What's next? Where is the breakthrough?"

I felt buried under expectations, responsibilities, and disappointments, but I couldn't stop moving. My kids still needed their mama. My clients still needed their therapist. The world still needed "Candice" even when I wasn't sure I had anything left to give.

The Pain Behind the Smile

People don't realize that depression doesn't always show up the way you think it will. It's not always tears, dark rooms, or staying in bed all day. Sometimes it's the exact opposite overfunctioning, perfectionism, and hyper-independence. It's answering, "I'm good" with a smile, even when you feel like you're unraveling inside. It's posting family photos where everyone looks happy, but the truth is you were crying in the bathroom 20 minutes before the camera clicked.

There were days I woke up and my body felt like lead. Days I went on autopilot, just moving through the checklist: get the kids to school, go to work, send emails, answer calls, make dinner, etc. Nobody would have known I was struggling because I wore "strength" like it was armor. But that armor was heavy. It wasn't protecting me, it was suffocating me.

And here's the thing: when you keep telling yourself, "I'm fine", you start believing that lie. You keep smiling while you're drowning. You start confusing survival with healing, busyness with progress. That's what I was doing, holding everything together so tightly, afraid that if I ever let go, everything would fall apart.

Grieving While Parenting

Let me say this clearly: being a parent while grieving is a whole different type of battle. It's waking up every day with a broken heart but still finding the strength to get the kids up and ready in the mornings, sign homework sheets during the week, pick kids up from after school activities, and spend time with them making memories. It's smiling through the pain so your kids don't feel it. It's lying with your face every single day.

I became a master at compartmentalizing my grief. I would wipe my tears before school drop-offs. I'd sit in parent-teacher conferences pretending to be "together" while my insides were a storm. And when my kids would ask where Daddy was, I'd reply, "He's downstairs," masking the ache of knowing that he wasn't really there, not for them, and not for me.

And when you're grieving while your co-parent is inconsistent, distant, or checked out, the pain doubles. Because now you're grieving two things: the relationship you lost and the partner who should have been there to lighten the load. I was grieving not just the man I married but the future I thought we were building together, the one where I wouldn't have to be everything for everyone, all the time.

KHAOS Reflection

In moments like these, the KHAOS Mindset taught me something powerful: **you can't RESET if you keep pretending you're okay. You literally can't heal what you refuse to acknowledge.**

Grief needs space.

Pain needs acknowledgment.

I had to stop hiding my sadness behind a smile and sit with it. I had to ask myself, *"What is this pain teaching me? What part of me needs healing?"*

That's what RESET is, Remember Every Situation Encourages Thought. Even the ones that shatter you. Especially the ones that shatter you.

When You Start Feeling Like a Ghost

There comes a point in a toxic or disconnected relationship when you stop feeling like a person and start feeling like a shadow, like a ghost in your own life. That's where I found myself. I was going through the motions. But inside, I was empty. My soul was tired in a way that no nap, no vacation, no self-care day could fix. It wasn't just that I was lonely, I was losing myself. I felt like the Candice I used to be was fading, replaced by this woman who was just making it happen every day.

We weren't fighting all the time, but we also weren't connected. We weren't a couple. We were roommates, co-existing under the same roof but living in separate worlds. The silence between us was deafening. We weren't laughing, dreaming, or building anymore. We were just... there. Frozen. Numb. Surrounded by unspoken resentments, broken promises, and years of unresolved hurt.

I remember looking at him one night, and for the first time, I didn't see "my husband." I saw someone who had become a stranger. Someone I loved deeply but could no longer reach. And the saddest part? I realized I had become a stranger to myself, too.

The Lie of Sticking It Out

I told myself I had to stay.

For the kids.

For the family.

Because my vows were " til death do us part." Because we had history, and history feels like a reason to hold on even when the present is killing you.

But the truth? Every single day, I was losing pieces of myself. The joyful version of me. The creative version. The soft, playful, "let's go on adventures" version. All of me was disappearing. And I had to ask myself the realest question I've ever asked:

"Why am I holding on to someone who doesn't make life easier?"

I sat with that question for weeks. I wrote it in my journal. I prayed about it. And every time, the same answer came back: *You're staying because you're afraid of what it means to heal and move forward.*

The KHAOS Mindset reminded me of something I had forgotten **FREE (Forgive, Release, Embrace, Elevate)** is not just about forgiving other people. It's about forgiving yourself for staying too long. Releasing the lies you told yourself about what love is supposed to look like. Embracing the truth, even when it hurts, and elevating beyond the cycle of pain.

RAW Reflection

Leaving wasn't easy. In fact, it was one of the hardest things I've ever done. But I had to get **RAW** with myself, Realize that I wasn't happy, Admit that I couldn't fix what I didn't break, and Work through the fear of starting over.

There's a freedom that comes when you stop betraying yourself just to keep someone else comfortable. A freedom that says, "I love me enough to choose me, even if it means walking away."

KHAOS Says: Honor the Sadness

Sadness isn't weakness. It's a signal. A message from your spirit that says, *"Pay attention. Something is off."* Too many of us have been taught to bury our sadness, to smile through it, to pray it away, to "stay strong" while it eats us alive. But KHAOS doesn't believe in bypassing pain.

In KHAOS, we **honor sadness** because it's often the doorway to clarity. When I stopped pretending I was fine and finally sat with my pain, I realized it wasn't just about my marriage failing. It was about years of carrying too much, years of silencing my own needs, years of confusing survival with love. Sadness was my spirit's way of saying, *"This isn't working. It's time to reset."*

RESET (Remember Every Situation Encourages Thought) taught me to look at my pain differently. Instead of asking, *"Why is this happening to me?"* I started asking, *"What is this teaching me?"* Every tear, every sleepless night, every silent cry in my car was shaping a stronger version of me, a version that would no longer beg to be chosen or stay where I wasn't valued.

KHAOS Check-In: When Sadness Speaks

- When did you first start feeling alone in your relationship?
- What emotions have you been hiding behind your smile?
- What's one thing your sadness is trying to tell you?
- How have you been surviving instead of healing?
- If your child came to you feeling like you feel, what would you say to them?

Take these questions seriously. Journal them. Sit with them. Because the truth is, **you can't heal what you won't face.**

RAW Reflection

You can't heal what you pretend doesn't hurt.

You can't grow in a garden where your joy keeps getting buried.

And you can't keep showing up for everyone else while abandoning yourself.

I had to give myself permission to fall apart so I could be put back together in a way that was whole, not just patched up. I had to **Realize** I was breaking. **Admit** that I deserved better. **Work through** the fear of stepping into a life where I was no longer defined by someone else's absence.

The KHAOS mindset taught me that healing isn't about fixing everything overnight, it's about being real with where you are, giving yourself grace, and taking one step at a time toward freedom. And when I finally gave myself that permission, the woman I had buried, the joyful, creative, vibrant me, started to heal and grow again.

Chapter 6

————··•••✕◈✕•••··————

Bargaining, Denial & False Hope

"I wasn't holding on to him. I was holding on to the story I told myself about us."

Before grief gives you clarity, it gives you confusion.

You start making deals in your mind.

"If I do this, maybe they'll change."

"If I can just hold on a little longer, they'll come back around."

"Maybe I'm the problem."

That's bargaining.

That's the mind's way of buying time before the heart is ready to accept the truth.

And in toxic relationships, bargaining doesn't just delay the inevitable… it traps you in cycles.

I Tried to Negotiate My Way Into Love

I prayed so many prayers.

"God, if this isn't meant for me, make him leave."

"God, help his words and his actions align."

"God, please help him see himself through your eyes."

I wasn't praying for peace.

I was praying for potential.

For possibility.

For a version of him that didn't exist anymore or maybe never did.

I wanted the fantasy more than I wanted the facts.

And that's the part that kept me stuck.

I'll never forget one of the hardest conversations we had while separated but still under the same roof. He looked at me and said, "I feel like I'm just your project. That's why we're together, you built your career off of our issues."

At first, it felt like a slap in the face. Like all the love, all the sacrifices, all the years we shared were reduced to some kind of case study. But part of me wondered... was there a little truth in it? Not that he was my project, but that I had poured so much into "fixing us" that it became my normal. My identity.

I was so busy trying to heal what was broken between us that I ignored how broken I was becoming. That conversation was another crack in the foundation. Because once someone says they feel like your project, you realize you can't heal them and you can't build a life with someone who resents the way you've held it together.

Denial Doesn't Always Look Like "No."

Sometimes It Sounds Like "Maybe."

I wasn't in denial because I didn't know what was going on.

I knew.

I knew about the lies.

The inconsistencies.

The shifts in energy.

The silence that spoke louder than words.

I was in denial because I didn't want it to be true.

I didn't want to start over.

I didn't want to admit that I built my life with someone who couldn't love me the way I needed to be loved.

I didn't want to believe I had wasted years… energy… pieces of myself.

So I created stories.

Excuses.

Illusions.

And I called it love.

But it wasn't love. It was fear wrapped in hope.

Hope Is Beautiful… Until It Becomes a Trap

Let me be clear: hope ain't the problem.

False hope is.

The kind that keeps you from seeing the truth.

The kind that convinces you that loyalty will change someone's character.

The kind that keeps you emotionally invested in a person who's already left the relationship in every way but physically.

Hope made me a prisoner.

I didn't want him, I wanted the version of him I thought he could become. The version I imagined in my head. The one who finally chose us and changed for our kids.

But every time I hoped for more… I got hurt worse.

Because the gap between who someone is and who you want them to be will break your heart every single time.

What You Ignore Today Will Destroy You Tomorrow

There were so many signs.

Little ones.

Big ones.

Loud ones.

Silent ones.

Times he didn't show up.

Times he made me feel small.

Times I caught him lying and made excuses for why I should stay.

I ignored them.

Dismissed them.

Told myself I was overreacting.

Told myself he "just needed time."

But all I was doing was prolonging the heartbreak.

When you live in denial, you start gaslighting yourself.

You stop trusting your intuition.

You stop honoring your needs.

You stop showing up for yourself.

That's what bargaining does.

It has you trying to prove you're worthy of someone who doesn't even value what you bring to the table.

The KHAOS Mindset and the Power of Surrender

In KHAOS, we don't beg people to stay.

We don't twist ourselves into knots to be chosen.

We get RAW and RESET.

Because at some point, you have to stop fighting for a relationship that's fighting against your peace.

You have to surrender, not because you're weak, but because holding on is breaking you.

Surrender says:

- "I see the truth now."
- "I may still love you, but I love me more."
- "I no longer want to fight for something that doesn't want to fight for me."

That's when healing starts.

The Science Behind the Struggle: Children exposed to high ACE (Adverse Childhood Experience) scores are more likely to form trauma bonds as adults. These bonds can mimic love but are rooted in survival. (CDC-Kaiser ACE Study)

(Quick Note on ACEs: ACEs, or Adverse Childhood Experiences, are the tough things we go through as kids like abuse, neglect, or living in a home with addiction, violence, or mental illness. They leave marks on how we see ourselves, trust others, and build relationships as adults.)

Truth From the Other Side

It wasn't until I realized he wasn't the only issue; I also held responsibility, that I started to heal.

He showed me exactly who he was, over and over again.

I just kept editing the story.

Kept casting him in a role he was never capable of playing.

Kept writing a love story that was never mutual.

His mouth said one thing, but his actions said another.

It was my wants… my fantasies… my denial… that kept me in bondage.

It wasn't until I accepted that he couldn't love me the way I needed because he didn't even love himself, that I could finally breathe.

I had to stop grieving the man I wished he could be…

And start accepting the man he actually was.

It was this realization that gave me the strength to tell him, "I love you, and will love you forever, but I'm no longer interested in the level of life you have to offer me and our children. At this point, I'm not even going to ask you to change, just know you can't keep doing THIS, with me."

KHAOS Check-In: Breaking the Bargain

- What lies have you told yourself to stay connected?
- What are you still holding on to that's already gone?
- Who do you keep rewriting in your mind just to justify staying?
- What truth are you afraid to face because of what it might mean?
- If you let go of the fantasy, what would freedom feel like?

RAW Reflection

The hardest part of healing is grieving the potential, the version of them you created in your head.

But once you stop bargaining and start accepting, you unlock the door to freedom.

You don't have to prove your worth to someone who refuses to see it.

You don't have to fight for a spot in a story that was never written for your joy.

Let go.

Not because it didn't matter...

But because you matter more.

At the end of the day, I had to grieve the loss of what I wanted so I could be open to embrace what I had, how it was impacting me, and figure out what I was gonna do with it.

Chapter 7

Acceptance "It Was Me"

"I wasn't mad at him anymore. I was mad at myself for lying to me for so long."

Acceptance doesn't come easy.

It doesn't show up with soft music and clarity in the sunlight.

It usually shows up after the crying, the chaos, and the questions that go unanswered.

It shows up when the blame has nowhere left to land, and all you're left with is a mirror.

I didn't get to acceptance by praying it into existence.

I got there by being **honest with myself in a way I had never been before.**

It wasn't him.

It was me.

It was the story I created.

The potential I saw.

The red flags I folded into origami and made look like love letters.

The Most Dangerous Lies Are the Ones We Tell Ourselves

I used to say, "He just needs time."

"He's been through a lot."

"He'll change."

"He's trying."

"We've been through worse."

But the truth was—I wasn't staying for him.

I was staying for *who I wanted him to be.*

I was in love with a future that didn't exist.

And the only reason I kept hurting… was because I kept choosing him over me.

Every time I ignored my needs.

Every time I swallowed my pain.

Every time I gave him another chance with no accountability.

That wasn't love. That was betrayal.

And not his, *mine.*

I Didn't Want Him to Change. I Wanted My Fantasy to Be Real.

It hit me one day like a gut punch:

He couldn't love me the way I needed to be loved — and he never could.

Not because I wasn't worthy.

Not because I didn't love hard enough.

But because he didn't have the capacity.

I saw him through eyes filled with hope, loyalty, and a desire to make it work.

But he couldn't see himself the way I did.

And I kept dragging us through a dream that wasn't mutual.

That's when I had to stop asking why he kept doing what he did…

And start asking *why I kept allowing it.*

That Wasn't His Role. That Was My Script.

I created a whole role for him in my life.

The supportive husband.

The healing father.

The partner who would finally choose me, completely.

But he never auditioned for that part, I just gave it to him.

He didn't study for it. He didn't prepare.

Hell, I don't know if he even wanted the role.

I cast him, scripted him, and expected him to perform in a story I was writing on my own.

And when he didn't follow the script, I got hurt.

But the truth is… he never knew how to play the role.

The Real Work Started When I Chose Me

Once I stopped trying to change him, I started changing me.

I had to get **RAW** with my patterns:

- Why I ignored the signs.
- Why I tolerated so much.
- Why I kept choosing people who didn't choose me back.

I had to sit in the discomfort of my decisions and not just his behavior.

I admitted my codependency.

My people-pleasing.

My addiction to potential.

My toxic loyalty to dysfunction dressed up as love.

And it hurt.

But that kind of hurt?

That's the pain that heals.

Forgiveness Doesn't Start With Them. It Starts With You.

When I let go of the blame, I finally found my power.

I forgave him.

Not because he deserved it...

But because I deserved peace.

I forgave myself.

For staying too long.

For trusting too deep.

For breaking my own heart trying to fix his.

And that's when it clicked:

I wasn't angry with him anymore.

I was angry with myself for lying to myself to keep the story alive.

But the minute I owned it, everything changed.

Not overnight. Not magically. But intentionally.

I started choosing me.

In small ways.

Then in bigger ones.

Then in ways that no longer required apology. I stopped waiting for others to choose me and chose myself.

The Science Behind the Struggle: *Betrayal trauma — especially from intimate partners — can result in symptoms similar to PTSD, including hypervigilance, emotional numbing, and dissociation. (Jennifer Freyd, University of Oregon)*

I Didn't Lose. I Learned.

That relationship taught me so much:

- About my capacity to love.
- About how long I'll fight for someone.
- About how strong I am.
- About how much healing I still had to do.

It also taught me this:

Sometimes love isn't enough.

Sometimes effort doesn't fix it.

Sometimes, the person you loved most is the one you have to leave to find yourself.

And that's okay.

Because I didn't lose. I learned.

And that lesson became the foundation of my freedom.

KHAOS Check-In: Acceptance and Accountability

- What were you trying to force to work that was already broken?
- What did you hope they'd become — and what did they actually show you?
- What role did you assign them that they never chose?
- Where have you abandoned yourself in the name of "trying one more time"?
- What truth do you need to accept so you can finally stop bleeding?

RAW Reflection:

Healing isn't about finding closure from them.

It's about closing the chapter within yourself.

It's about telling the truth — even when it hurts.

Not "they did this to me."

But "I saw who they were and still stayed... now I choose differently."

This is where the power comes back.

This is where you rebuild.

You didn't fail. You just finished.

And on the other side of acceptance, there's a better version of you.

PART III: THE REBIRTH

Chapter 8

From CHAOS to KHAOS

"I couldn't help acting out severely because I never learned how to FEEL safe."

Before I actually walked through and understood the KHAOS Mindset, I was a CHAOS kid.

And I don't mean the kind of chaos people talk about casually like, "Oh, you're a little wild."

No, I mean **Couldn't Help Acting Out Severely.**

Because that's what happens when you grow up emotionally neglected, emotionally abused, and emotionally confused.

That's what happens when you're raised in survival mode.

That's what happens when trauma becomes your teacher.

Survival Looks Different on Everybody

For some people, survival looks like shutting down.

For me, survival looked like:

- Lying to avoid conflict.
- Freezing my emotions to feel safe.
- Overperforming to earn approval.

- Internalizing everything because speaking up wasn't safe.
- Exploding after holding it in too long.

I was a whole adult before I realized how much my childhood impacted how I moved in relationships.

I didn't understand boundaries because nobody taught me I was allowed to have them.

I didn't know how to express emotions because every time I tried, I got punished or dismissed.

I didn't feel safe in love because love was unstable, conditional, and sometimes cruel.

So when I got into adult relationships, I showed up with the emotional toolkit of a child who had learned to survive.

And that's what so many of us are doing: *surviving relationships instead of experiencing them.*

Emotional Injuries That Nobody Saw

You can't heal what you never name.

So let's name it.

We talk about trauma in terms of events, abuse, loss, and violence.

But trauma is also:

- Being shamed for expressing emotions.
- Having your needs consistently unmet.
- Learning love through fear or silence.
- Being praised for being strong when you're actually struggling.

These emotional injuries don't just disappear.

They evolve.

They become your internal wiring.

And if left unchecked, they start choosing for you.

Who you love.

What you tolerate.

When you speak.

How you cope.

Your trauma becomes your compass until you decide to recalibrate.

When I Met Me Again: The KHAOS Shift

The day I decided to stop surviving and start healing… that was the day I met myself again.

Not the version I became to make people comfortable.

Not the strong Black woman version that didn't cry.

Not the overgiving version that lost herself in relationships.

But the real me.

The one who was still in there… waiting.

The one who was tired of living in emotional survival mode.

The one who deserved safety, not silence.

And that's when I shifted from CHAOS to KHAOS.

What Is KHAOS?

KHAOS is not just a mindset, it's a **movement**.

It's a roadmap out of toxic patterns and into emotional liberation.

KHAOS = Keep Healing And Overcoming Struggles

It teaches you that healing is not a destination, it's a lifestyle.

It's not always loud. It's not always pretty. But it's always necessary.

When you're in KHAOS, you don't just cope, you confront.

You don't just survive, you shift.

KHAOS gave me language. It gave me tools. It gave me back my power.

And the first tool it gave me was **RAW.**

The RAW Process: Realize. Admit. Work Through.

Let's be real: healing starts with honesty because accountability is at the root of healing.

Not honesty for the 'Gram.

Not honesty in your group chat.

But the kind of honesty that hits you in your chest.

REALIZE where the patterns started.

ADMIT how they're impacting you (and how you're helping keep them alive).

WORK THROUGH what no longer serves the person you're becoming.

I had to get RAW with myself:

- About why I stayed.
- About how I showed up.
- About how trauma shaped my expectations.

And that shit hurt.

But it was the beginning of everything.

The Science Behind the Struggle: *Parental functioning is directly impacted by unresolved grief. Children of grieving* *parents often exhibit increased anxiety and emotional dysregulation. (Journal of Family Psychology, 2020)*

I Didn't Need to Be Perfect. I Needed to Be Present.

I spent years trying to fix everything outside of me:

The man. The house. The kids. The business.

But what I really needed?

To sit with myself.

To feel what I'd been avoiding.

To listen to what my body had been screaming.

You can't heal in the same environment that broke you.

And you can't be present for your life if you're still haunted by your past.

KHAOS taught me how to breathe again.

How to regulate.

How to not just react, but respond.

I finally stopped acting out and started acting in alignment.

Your CHAOS Isn't Who You Are. It's Where You Started.

If you've ever said, "I'm just like this" pause.

You're not just angry.

You're unhealed.

You're not just cold.

You're protecting yourself.

You're not just "too much."

You've just never had space to be seen as you are.

Your CHAOS was never your identity.

It was your survival strategy.

And you don't have to keep wearing it.

You get to shift.

You get to grow.

You get to evolve into someone who doesn't have to beg to be loved right.

KHAOS Check-In: From Surviving to Healing

- What does emotional survival look like for you?
- What patterns from your childhood still show up in your relationships?
- How do you respond when you feel unsafe emotionally?
- Are you reacting from your present… or your past?

- What would your life look like if you chose to keep healing instead of just surviving?

RAW Reflection:

You don't have to stay stuck in what hurt you.

You don't have to repeat what raised you.

You don't have to carry the pain that was passed down to you.

You get to choose KHAOS.

You get to keep healing and overcoming, for real this time.

Because the you that's coming… is worth every tear, every boundary, and every shift.

This is your becoming.

Chapter 9

RESET & Reclaiming Self

"The past had me in a chokehold... but I remembered, I don't live there anymore."

When life breaks you down, it doesn't just leave you broken, it leaves you scattered. Pieces of you spread out across memories, moments, and people who didn't protect them.

And one day you look up and realize:

You've been functioning, but you haven't really been living.

You've been reacting instead of creating.

Performing instead of feeling.

Surviving instead of healing.

That's where RESET comes in.

What Is RESET?

RESET is the KHAOS process of reclaiming yourself.

It stands for:

Remember Every Situation Encourages Thought.

RESET is how you:

- Unlearn who trauma told you to be.
- Remember who you actually are.
- Begin again, not from scratch, but from wisdom.

It's not about pretending it didn't happen.

It's about choosing how you show up now that it did.

The Past Doesn't Get to Dictate the Present

For a long time, I lived in emotional autopilot.

Triggered by tone.

Shut down by rejection.

Afraid of softness.

Comfortable in chaos.

My nervous system had been trained to expect pain. So even peace made me anxious.

But once I saw the pattern, I couldn't unsee it.

Once I understood the wound, I couldn't ignore it.

And once I realized **I don't live there anymore**… I gave myself permission to create a new normal.

Reclaiming Self Looks Like:

- Saying "no" without explaining.

- Not calling someone back just because you're lonely.
- Choosing silence over defending yourself to someone committed to misunderstanding you.
- Not internalizing someone's inability to love you.
- Doing something for you that isn't about proving, fixing, or earning anything.

Reclaiming self doesn't mean becoming someone new.

It means returning to the version of you that existed before you were told you weren't enough.

It means reminding your spirit:

"you are enough as you are."

The Healing Isn't Linear — But It's Worth It

Some days I felt strong.

Other days I backslid.

Some nights I missed the familiarity, even if it was toxic.

But the difference was: I didn't unpack and stay there anymore.

I let myself feel it.

I let the tears come.

I let the guilt visit — but I didn't invite it to move back in.

Because every time I RESET, I got closer to my truth.

And that truth was:

I am not who they told me I was.

I am not what they did to me.

I am not a reflection of the pain I survived.

The Science Behind the Struggle: *Repetition compulsion — the unconscious drive to reenact familiar trauma — is often what keeps people stuck in cycles of toxic relationships. (Sigmund Freud, later confirmed by modern trauma research)*

The Science Behind the Struggle: *Traumatic loss and betrayal can activate the brain's threat system, particularly the amygdala, making it harder to regulate emotions and trust again. (Harvard Health, 2018)*

You Can't Build a New Life With an Old Mindset

I had to unlearn everything that taught me survival was love.

I had to learn:

- That stillness wasn't laziness.
- That peace didn't mean boredom.
- That healthy love doesn't feel like walking on eggshells.
- That my worth wasn't up for negotiation.

RESET isn't a one-time event.

It's a practice.

A discipline.

A decision you make every single day to show up as the healed version of you, even when the wounded version wants to lead.

The Moment I Chose Me

There was a moment. A quiet one.

No tears. No breakdown. Just a choice.

I looked in the mirror and said:

"I will no longer be a prisoner of my own mind. Mentally, physically, emotionally, spiritually, and financially, I will be free, I will be ME."

That's when the shift happened.

Not because he changed.

Not because the past didn't hurt anymore.

But because I finally believed I was worthy of more than surviving.

KHAOS Check-In: Reclaiming Self

- What old beliefs are you still living by that no longer serve you?

- Who do you become when you feel unsafe? And who are you when you feel seen?
- What part of your identity was shaped by pain instead of purpose?
- When was the last time you chose you without guilt?
- If you could RESET your life starting now, what would that version of you need?

RAW Reflection:

Your trauma might've shaped your story, but it doesn't get to finish it.

You do.

Reclaiming yourself means grieving who you had to become to survive and honoring who you're becoming to finally live.

This is your RESET.

This is your return.

This is you, choosing to rebuild from love, not loss.

Chapter 10

FREE to Be

"I didn't just leave the relationship, I left the version of me who needed it."

There's something sacred about walking away without anger.

Not because you're unbothered, but because you've made peace with the parts of you that kept going back.

That's what the FREE process gave me:

Forgive. Release. Embrace. Elevate.

It became the final part of my KHAOS healing, the part where I didn't just grieve the loss... I grew from it.

Because real freedom ain't about being over it, it's about no longer being owned by it.

FORGIVE: Yourself First

Let me say this clearly:

You don't have to forgive people to invite them back into your life.

You forgive so they no longer live in your head rent-free.

But before I could forgive him, I had to forgive **me.**

For not leaving sooner.

For believing the lies.

For silencing my intuition.

For betraying myself to keep someone else comfortable.

For breaking my own heart, hoping they'd stop breaking it for me.

I had to forgive the version of me that didn't know better, and I had to stop punishing the version of me who finally does.

RELEASE: The Weight of the "What Ifs"

I held on to so many "what ifs":

- What if he changes?
- What if I'm making a mistake?
- What if I never find love again?
- What if the kids hate me for walking away?
- What if I miss him later?

But here's what I learned:

The "what ifs" will keep you shackled to a life that no longer fits.

They will convince you to stay where your spirit is suffocating.

They will have you dragging dead relationships into new seasons.

I had to let go.

Not because I didn't love him anymore…

But because I finally loved me more than I feared walking away. I realized I knew what it felt like to hurt and hold on and understood I deserved to know what it felt like to heal and move forward.

EMBRACE: The Real, Raw, Rebuilt You

The version of me that emerged after the storm?

She's not polished.

She's not perfect.

She's not all-knowing.

But she's **real.**

She's **intentional.**

She's **free.**

I don't beg to be chosen anymore.

I don't shrink to keep the peace.

I don't abandon myself to avoid abandonment.

I *feel now.*

I *ask for what I need now.*

I *choose softness without fear now.*

I embrace me, all of me. The woman I was, the one I am, and the one I'm still becoming.

ELEVATE: You Didn't Just Survive... You Transformed

Elevation isn't about glowing up for Instagram.

It's not about revenge or proving anything to anyone.

Elevation is internal.

It's peace that can't be snatched.

It's knowing you'll never go back to what broke you, not out of bitterness, but because you're no longer available for that version of life.

I didn't just survive a divorce.

I survived myself.

I survived my patterns.

My denial.

My pain tolerance.

My fantasy of love that kept me in cycles of suffering.

And now?

I rise, not because I never fell, but because I learned how to stand up different.

Grief Gave Me Me

People talk about grief like it's a thief.

But in my case, it was a mirror.

It showed me what I ignored.

It forced me to feel what I had buried.

It handed me the pieces of myself I didn't even know I had lost.

And in the ashes of everything I thought I needed... I found me.

Not the performative version.

Not the broken-down caretaker.

Not the anxious little girl trying to be enough.

Just me. Whole. Present. Powerful. Free.

KHAOS Check-In: FREE to Be

- What do you need to forgive yourself for?
- What emotional weight are you still carrying that's no longer yours?
- Who do you become when you no longer need to prove you're worthy?

- What are you finally ready to release so you can embrace peace?
- What does your elevated self need from you right now?

RAW Reflection:

This ain't the end of your story.

It's the beginning of your becoming.

You get to forgive.

You get to release.

You get to embrace all of you, even the parts you once hid.

You get to elevate, not in spite of the pain, but because you chose to heal through it.

This is what it means to break **FREE.**

This is what it means to survive when the world around you dies, and still rise anyway.

I gotta be honest, even as I accepted what was, I had to learn how to live in this new space without rushing the healing. That's where I learned how to be PATIENT.

Chapter 11

Learning to Be PATIENT With Yourself

One of the hardest things about grief is that it doesn't move on your timeline. Healing isn't linear. Some days you feel strong, and other days you wonder if you'll ever feel like yourself again. That's why the PATIENT skill is one of the most important parts of the KHAOS Mindset.

PATIENT stands for: Pause And Think, Inhale/Exhale, Now Talk or Tap Out.

It's a tool we use to ground ourselves in emotionally overwhelming moments. Because grief is disorienting. You can go from numb to enraged in 30 seconds, and back again. Being PATIENT with yourself means honoring the ebb and flow of that process and building your capacity to self-regulate, reflect, and reset without shame.

After the divorce, I had to learn how to breathe again. For real. I had spent so long holding it all in that I forgot what it felt like to exhale. To be still. To *feel* without needing to perform or protect. Being PATIENT meant giving myself permission to grieve on my terms, in my own time.

There were moments I had to walk out of rooms and cry in the hallway, bathroom, or car. There were moments I screamed into pillows or stayed in bed longer than I wanted to. But the turning point came when I realized that those moments didn't make me weak, they made me *human*.

Practicing PATIENT helped me start responding to my emotions instead of reacting from them. It taught me to ask: What am I really feeling? What do I need in this moment? Is it space? Support? Stillness? And it reminded me that tapping out doesn't mean giving up, it means honoring your limits so you can come back stronger.

This skill is also what helped me model regulation for my children. When they were melting down from their own grief, I had to be the example. I had to *be* the calm I wanted them to feel. And some days, I wasn't. But the more I practiced, the better I got at it.

Being PATIENT with yourself isn't soft. It's strength. It's discipline. It's choosing healing even when you want to run. And when your world has been turned upside down, it's one of the most powerful choices you can make.

KHAOS Check-In: Learning to be PATIENT with You

- Where do you notice impatience in your healing?
- What's one thing you can give yourself grace for today?
- Are you allowing space to feel without rushing the fix?

RAW Reflection:

Healing is not a race.

There's no gold medal for pretending to be okay.

Take your time, your peace is not on a deadline.

Chapter 12

Life After the Papers – Rebuilding When Everything Is Broken

Walking away from someone you love physically hurts.

It's literally the death of a union, a bond, a shared world. Going to court on the day of the divorce felt like viewing the body at the funeral. You don't want to see it through, but you know you have to for closure. It was the last chapter of a long, painful book I didn't want to finish, but couldn't keep reading either.

No one prepares you for what happens after the papers are signed.

Nobody talks about the gut punch that comes when you wake up in a house that feels unfamiliar, not because the walls changed, but because the energy did. He was gone. I had fought for the marriage, fought for the family, and now... it was just me. I thought I'd be relieved. But it felt like I was dying a slow, painful death. Grief came in waves. There were days I couldn't breathe. Days I prayed for God to just make the pain stop.

And then came the question I couldn't run from:

"What the fuck am I supposed to do now?"

The answer was simple, but painful: Rebuild. Create a new normal.

But I didn't know where to start. I had lost so much of myself trying to hold everything together that I had to go searching for pieces of me I hadn't seen in years. I was scared, unsure, and exhausted. I didn't know what I wanted anymore. I had to figure out who I was without him, without "us," without the titles and routines that once made me feel grounded.

I had to learn how to build a new normal.

But grief doesn't stop just because the relationship ends. It keeps knocking. Memories become landmines. You sit in your kitchen and wonder how to cook for one less. You look around the house and feel like a guest in your own life. You try to explain the change to people who only knew you as part of a pair, and they offer surface-level support that never really touches the pain.

And here's the truth: I missed him… even though he hurt me.

That's what people don't understand about trauma bonds. You miss the familiarity, not necessarily the love. You miss the routine, the rhythm, the illusion. There were moments I questioned my decision. I asked myself if I made it all up, if I exaggerated the hurt, if I could've held on just a little longer.

But therapy saved me from going back to a burning house.

I found myself in that space. I gave myself permission to tell the truth. I stopped trying to be strong and started being honest. I cried without apology. I screamed. I sat in silence. I got real.

Therapy didn't fix me, it gave me space to fix myself. It reminded me I didn't ruin anything. I simply outgrew it.

When He Came Back

He came to me a few times after the divorce was final, after the damage had already been done and told me he wanted to try again. That he loved me. That he was sorry. That things would be different this time. But by then, I had already buried the version of me who had a desire to live life with him. I wasn't interested in repeating a cycle that almost cost me my joy. I saw the love for what it was: conditional, convenient, and rooted in comfort, not commitment.

And I told him the truth.

"You love me selfishly because you want me with you even if I'm not happy.. But I love you unselfishly. I want you to be happy... even if that happiness doesn't include me."

That was the moment I knew I had finally let go. Not just of the relationship, but of the version of myself who would've accepted that kind of love. I didn't need to be wanted. I needed to be well. And anything that cost me my peace couldn't be apart of my testimony going forward.

One of the hardest things about healing is accepting that love isn't always enough.

We loved each other. But we also hurt each other. Repeatedly. And love without accountability is chaos. I was tired of surviving. I wanted to live. I wanted to build a life I didn't need to escape from.

So I took it one day at a time.

I started by reclaiming small parts of my life. I lit candles, moved into a new house, took vacations, and built my relationship with myself. I got quiet enough to hear myself again. I practiced the RESET skill: Remember Every Situation Encourages Thought. I stopped letting my pain think for me. I became intentional about who I allowed into my space, what energy I gave my attention to, and what boundaries I kept in place.

There were setbacks, of course. Days where I didn't get out of bed. Nights where loneliness wrapped around me like a weighted blanket Spaces where binge eating and isolation dwelled. But there were also moments of joy. Moments where I laughed from my gut. Moments where I saw glimpses of a woman I hadn't seen in years.

I started to believe I wasn't a failure because my family was broken. I wasn't out for the count. I was just getting started.

Rebuilding after a breakup, especially a marriage, isn't linear. It's messy. It's sacred. And it's yours. I had to learn to forgive myself for what I tolerated. For what I allowed. For what I wanted so badly to work. I had to grieve the life I thought I would have, the dreams I had to bury, and the version of myself that no longer fit the woman I was becoming.

I stopped trying to go back to what was.

I started creating what could be.

And that became my power. My peace. My promise to myself.

I didn't just survive the divorce, I survived losing me.

KHAOS Check-In: Life After

- What part of your old normal are you still grieving?
- Have you given yourself space to feel the grief that came after the divorce or break up, not just during it?
- What expectations did you have about healing that you're now realizing weren't real?

RAW Reflection:

Grief doesn't end when the papers are signed.

Sometimes the real pain starts after the closure.

And that's okay. Keep breathing. Keep healing. Keep choosing you.

Chapter 13

Parenting Through Pain – Helping My Kids Grieve Him While Healing Me

Parenting through grief is one of the hardest things I've ever had to do. I wasn't just grieving the loss of a marriage, I was guiding two children through their own losses. Loss of structure, safety, presence, and consistency. He didn't just abandon me, he abandoned us.

He became a text message dad. A ghost with a phone number. The kind of father who popped in when it was convenient, who made promises and rarely followed through. At first, I tried to shield the kids from it. I wanted to protect their image of him. But they weren't blind. They felt the absence.

My daughter was angry. Not just at him, at me. After the divorce, he fed her lies and twisted the narrative, convincing her I was the one who ruined our family. For a while, she believed it. And for a moment, I felt like I lost her too. Our relationship became tense, disconnected. We stopped laughing. We barely talked. I was grieving my marriage and my bond with my baby girl all at once.

And still, I had to show up. I couldn't fall apart. I had to be mother and father, nurturer and protector, therapist and teacher while trying to heal myself. I didn't get the luxury of falling apart, even when I was gasping for air on the inside. I had to *reparent myself* while parenting them. I had to break generational patterns while holding my family together.

We stopped doing a lot of things as a family in those early days. Even simple routines like eating together became foreign. The house felt hollow. He was gone physically, but his presence lingered, through anger, confusion, and silence. And still, I had to keep moving. I had to keep leading.

Therapy, prayer, and embracing our village became a lifeline. For all of us.

We each needed space to process and tools to cope. My daughter needed help living in the spaces she could control. My son needed help understanding his father's absence wasn't his fault. And I needed help remembering who I was outside of survival. Therapy gave us that. I learned to parent from a healed space instead of a hurt one. I also released guilt and learned how to shift from reacting to responding.

Over time, things got better. Not perfect. Not neat. But better.

We started eating together again. Not because we were pretending everything was okay, but because we were learning how to be okay. We created new habits, new memories, new meaning. And slowly, we began to heal. Seven years later, my daughter is now in college studying to become a teacher. My son is excelling in his freshman year of high school. They are resilient, wise, grounded. They see the truth of who their father is, and they've learned to manage their expectations with love, compassion and clarity.

We're not pretending. We're not performing. We're living in our truth.

They are living examples of what it means to Keep Healing And Overcoming Struggles. We talk about our feelings. We name our needs. We validate each other. We set boundaries. We rest. We repair. We grow.

Parenting through pain didn't destroy us, it refined us.

We are not broken. We are healing, growing, and creating our new normal. We are living a life of KHAOS daily!

KHAOS Check-In: Parenting through the pain

- How has your grief impacted the way you parent?
- Are you showing up for your kids while still trying to show up for yourself?
- What's one thing your children have taught you about healing?

RAW Reflection:

You can be a present parent and still feel broken.

You can teach your children resilience while still finding your own.

You are doing better than you think and they see you even when you don't see yourself.

What Grief Revealed: A Clinician's Reflection

I didn't just live this. I studied it. I sat with it. And eventually… I healed through it.

As a therapist, I've walked with countless people through grief, betrayal, and emotional unraveling. But nothing in my clinical training prepared me for what it would feel like to be in it, to be the one on the floor, gasping for air after a relationship I fought so hard to keep finally collapsed.

This wasn't just a divorce. It was an emotional crash built on a shaky foundation of unhealed trauma, high ACE scores, attachment wounds, and years of normalizing emotional abandonment.

I didn't realize it then, but I wasn't just grieving a relationship. I was grieving every version of myself that had ever accepted being invisible.

I was grieving the little girl in me who learned that being strong meant staying silent.

That love meant loyalty, even when it hurt. That showing up for others was more important than showing up for yourself.

The trauma didn't start with the marriage. It started long before in environments where survival was prioritized over safety, where feelings weren't validated, where emotional regulation wasn't taught, just expected.

My **ACEs** weren't just numbers on a list, they were my *blueprint*. They shaped how I chose partners, how I gave love, how I stayed too long, and how I tolerated too much.

So I became the strong one. The fixer. The nurturer. The freezer and fawner. The one who kept the house together while silently falling apart. And that "strong friend" identity? It was a trauma response dressed up as a personality trait.

And he had trauma too. Different wounds, but just as deep. His need for validation, control, and avoidance didn't come out of nowhere. He was also shaped by pain.

By secrets. By emotional suppression that taught him to run when things got real.

To isolate instead of communicate. To escape instead of confront.

But while I chose to face mine, he continued to run from his.

And when two unhealed people try to love each other without tools or truth, it turns into performance. A performance of partnership. Of family. Of connection.

But beneath the surface, it's all breaking.

From a clinical perspective, our relationship was a case study in:

- **Attachment trauma:** I clung, he withdrew.
- **Codependency:** I overfunctioned, hoping it would create closeness.
- **Emotional abandonment:** Both given and received.
- **Trauma reenactment:** Playing out old wounds, expecting new outcomes.
- **Survival-mode bonding:** Built not on peace, but on the need to not be alone.

If I hadn't done the work…

I would've kept performing healing while secretly bleeding.

But I chose to stop the cycle.

I chose to look at my pain, not just pathologize it.

I chose to use the tools I created for others… on myself.

That's where **KHAOS** came in.

KHAOS, *Keep Healing And Overcoming Struggles*, was born before the divorce, but during the aftermath, it became my oxygen.

- **RAW** helped me stop lying to myself about what I felt, what I feared, and what I allowed.
- **RESET** gave me permission to reflect instead of react, and stop replaying old arguments trying to rewrite the past.
- **PATIENT** reminded me that I didn't have to prove my pain to be worthy of peace.
- **FREE** gave me the courage to forgive, not to excuse — but to finally release myself.

If I hadn't done this work, I would've passed the blueprint on. To my children. To my clients. To myself. And that wouldn't have been fair to any of us. At the end of the day, accountability is at the root of healing, and as a healer, I have to do my due diligence to walk it like I talk it and practice what I preach. I am not only a teacher of KHAOS but a student as well.

This book is the evidence that **healing is possible.** But it's also a reminder that healing is necessary.

Because trauma will trick you into performing wholeness while silently self-destructing.

And this isn't just my story.

It's the story of every person who has been taught to carry it all, hold it in, and keep it cute.

The people who've been applauded for being strong, but never asked if they were okay.

The ones who confuse suffering with loyalty and struggle with love.

The ones who are breaking generational contracts in silence.

This isn't just about my healing. It's about ours.

If this is your story, or even just a piece of it, let this be your confirmation.

You are not too broken. You are not too late. You are not too far gone.

We can feel it and still be free.

We can grieve and still grow.

We can rewrite the blueprint and break the cycle as we Keep Healing And Overcoming Struggles.

Remember, happiness, healing, and peace are inside jobs, you gotta do the work!

Closing letter: From My Heart to Yours

If you've made it to this moment, pause and take a breath.

A real one. Deep. Intentional.

Inhale who you've become.

Exhale who you had to let go to get here.

This wasn't just a book.

It was a mirror. A confession. A reckoning. A release.

It was the tear-streaked journal you didn't know you needed.

It was the late-night talk with a friend who finally gets it.

And most of all, it was proof, proof that grief doesn't get the final word.

I wrote this through the lens of divorce, but let's be clear:

This is for anyone who's had to grieve the living.

For anyone who's had to mourn a mother still breathing, a friend who stopped showing up, a love that couldn't meet you where you grew.

If you've ever poured from a soul that stayed thirsty, this was for you too.

Because I know what it feels like to perform life with a shattered heart.

To answer emails and make dinner and raise babies while silently falling apart.

To question your worth because someone else couldn't see it.

To carry guilt for choosing yourself after years of betraying your own peace.

But I need you to know this:

- You are not broken.
- You are not too late.
- You are not hard to love.
- You are creating a new normal.

The loss? It wasn't your ending, it was your awakening.

You've learned to forgive people who never apologized.

To love people from afar.

To choose peace over performance.

And to hold yourself like nobody else ever did.

So here's what I pray for you:

- I pray you give yourself grace, even on the days you feel stuck.
- I pray you never again trade your sanity for a seat at someone else's table.

- I pray you fall so in love with your healing that anything less than joy feels foreign

- And I pray you remember this: everything you thought was breaking you… was actually building you.

You're still here. Still rising. Still choosing you.

This is not the end. This is *the beginning of your new normal.* And this time you're not gonna play about you!

With love and compassion,

Dr. Candice E. Cox, LCSW, CATP, CCTP

KHAOS Healing Toolkit: RAW – RESET – FREE

Full toolkit content including RAW, RESET, and FREE exercises...

🔥 Reflect. Release. Rebuild.

Take a moment to pause. What's coming up for you?

- What moment in your life made everything feel like it was falling apart?
- How did you first recognize that the relationship was no longer healthy?
- What truths have you been avoiding that you're ready to face?

🔥 Reflect. Release. Rebuild.

Take a moment to pause. What's coming up for you?

- What made you the angriest during your loss or breakup?
- Who or what have you been protecting with your silence?
- What does your anger want you to know?

◢ Reflect. Release. Rebuild.

Take a moment to pause. What's coming up for you?

- When did you first realize you were emotionally carrying too much?
- What do you miss about your past relationship — even if it wasn't healthy?
- How did you learn to numb or hide your emotions growing up?

◢ Reflect. Release. Rebuild.

Take a moment to pause. What's coming up for you?

- What 'deals' did you try to make with yourself or your partner?
- What were you afraid to lose if you let go?
- How has your need for control shown up in your healing?

◢ Reflect. Release. Rebuild.

Take a moment to pause. What's coming up for you?

- What warning signs did you ignore?
- When did you realize that things were never going back to how they were?
- What role did denial play in keeping you connected?

⚓ Reflect. Release. Rebuild.

Take a moment to pause. What's coming up for you?

- What truth about your relationship or yourself hurt the most to admit?
- In what ways were you trying to rewrite someone else's story to fit your needs?
- What does forgiveness — for them and for you — look like today?

⚓ Reflect. Release. Rebuild.

Take a moment to pause. What's coming up for you?

- Who did your ex remind you of?
- What patterns from childhood did you repeat in your adult relationships?
- What did your family teach you — directly or indirectly — about love and pain?

⚓ Reflect. Release. Rebuild.

Take a moment to pause. What's coming up for you?

- What patterns do you keep returning to that no longer serve you?
- How has staying in "familiar" kept you stuck?

- What version of yourself are you finally ready to let go of?

♨ Reflect. Release. Rebuild.

Take a moment to pause. What's coming up for you?

- What happens inside you when someone breaks your trust?
- How did you teach people to treat you in past relationships?
- What does rebuilding trust in yourself look like now?

♨ Reflect. Release. Rebuild.

Take a moment to pause. What's coming up for you?

- How did grief impact your ability to show up as a parent or caregiver?
- What lies did you tell yourself to get through the day?
- What kind of support do you deserve but haven't been asking for?

What Now? — Building the New You

You've grieved the loss. You've cried, screamed, journaled, doubted, and grown. And now you're here, staring at the space between what was and what could be.

This is the most important part.

Grief doesn't end. It evolves. You're not trying to get back to who you were before — that version of you doesn't exist anymore. You're becoming someone new. Someone more whole. More present. More honest.

Here's where you begin:

🔑 1. Reconnect with your body.

Your body holds every memory — the betrayal, the numbness, the moments you didn't speak up. It also holds your healing. Start by listening to what your body needs. Rest. Movement. Pleasure. Nourishment. Let it lead you back to safety.

🔧 2. Build your emotional toolbox.

Practice your KHAOS tools daily — RAW, RESET, PATIENT, and FREE aren't just acronyms. They're rituals.

- RAW: Get honest about your patterns. Realize what's real, Admit what hurts, and Work through what's been weighing you down.

- RESET: Ground yourself. Interrupt the loops. Remember that Every Situation Encourages Thought.
- PATIENT: Pause before reacting. Inhale/Exhale. Then choose how to respond.
- FREE: Choose peace. Forgive, Release, Embrace, and Elevate. That's how you move forward.

🧱 3. Create a life that doesn't require survival mode.

You don't need to be strong all the time. You don't need to be "on" all the time. Start building routines, relationships, and environments that support your softness — not just your strength.

💬 4. Tell the truth — even when it shakes things up.

The more you speak your truth, the more space you create for healing. The more you advocate for your needs, the more you disrupt the cycle. Healing starts where honesty lives.

📬 5. Love yourself loud.

Not just in words. In action. In boundaries. In rest. In how you talk to yourself when no one's listening. The version of you who begged for scraps deserves a love that feels like home.

Your life is not over. It's just beginning — on your terms.

You are not who you were before the loss. You are someone who knows grief and grace at the same time. That's power.

The KHAOS Mindset Affirmation

Speak this over yourself as often as you need to. Healing starts with what you believe.

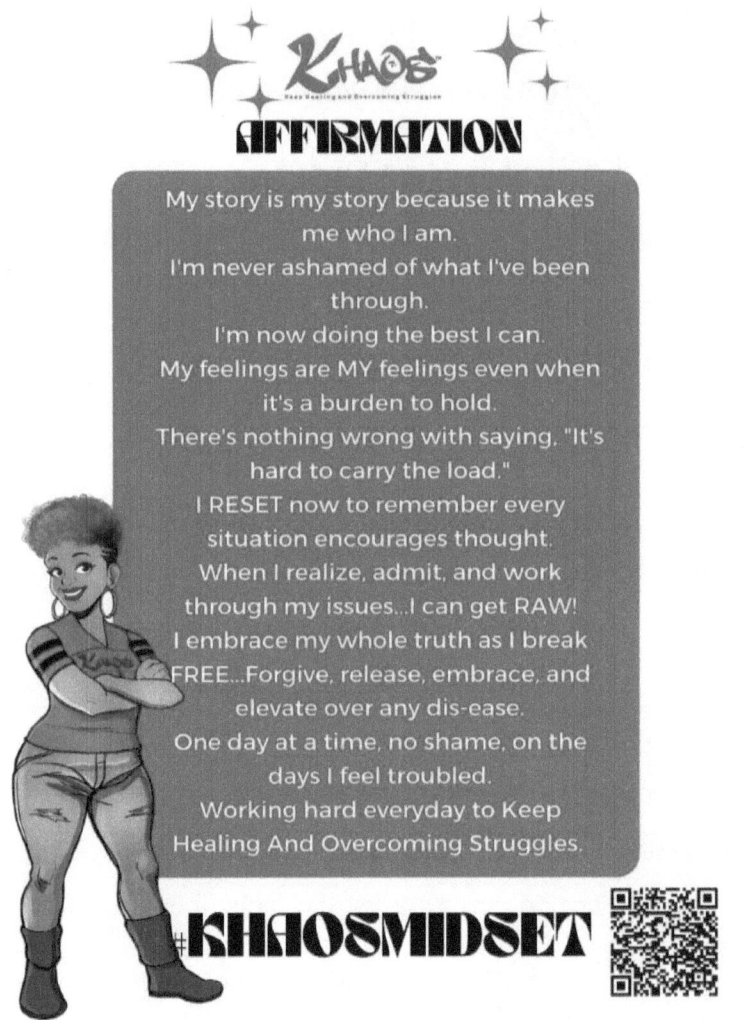

Scan the QR code to follow the KHAOS Mindset

and connect with Dr. Cox

Real Talk Glossary

ACEs (Adverse Childhood Experiences)

These are the tough things you went through as a kid — like abuse, neglect, or growing up in chaos. ACEs leave emotional fingerprints on how you love, trust, and show up in relationships.

Here are the 10 original ACE questions to help you understand your own ACE score:

(Answer "Yes" for each one that applies to your life before age 18.)

1. Did a parent or other adult in the household often or very often swear at you, insult you, put you down, or humiliate you? Or act in a way that made you afraid you might be physically hurt?

2. Did a parent or other adult in the household often or very often push, grab, slap, or throw something at you? Or ever hit you so hard that you had marks or were injured?

3. Did an adult or person at least 5 years older than you ever touch or fondle you or have you touch their body in a sexual way? Or attempt or actually have oral, anal, or vaginal intercourse with you?

4. Did you often or very often feel that no one in your family loved you or thought you were important or special? Or

that your family didn't look out for each other, feel close to each other, or support each other?

5. Did you often or very often feel that you didn't have enough to eat, had to wear dirty clothes, or had no one to protect you? Or that your parents were too drunk or high to take care of you or take you to the doctor if needed?

6. Was a biological parent ever lost to you through divorce, abandonment, or other separation?

7. Was your mother or stepmother often or very often pushed, grabbed, slapped, or had something thrown at her? Or was she sometimes or often kicked, bitten, hit with a fist, or hit with something hard? Or ever repeatedly hit over at least a few minutes or threatened with a gun or knife?

8. Did you live with anyone who was a problem drinker or alcoholic, or who used street drugs?

9. Was a household member depressed or mentally ill, or did a household member attempt suicide?

10. Did a household member go to prison?

Your ACE Score: Add up your "Yes" answers. The higher the number, the greater your risk for long-term emotional and physical health struggles — but it's also a roadmap for healing. Your score doesn't define you. Healing changes everything.

Trauma Bond

That intense, "can't let go even though it's hurting me" connection you feel with someone. It's not healthy love it's survival dressed up like loyalty.

Emotional Casualties

The hidden losses and wounds you carry from a relationship, breakup, or traumatic experience. It's not just the relationship ending, it's the emotional fallout that stays with you if you don't heal it.

Toxic Loyalty

Being loyal to someone simply because of the role they play in your life (partner, family member, friend), even when their behavior hurts you. It's that "ride or die" mentality that ends up killing your peace instead of building your joy.

KHAOS (Keep Healing And Overcoming Struggles)

The mindset that saved me — and the one I hope saves you too. It's about being honest with yourself, reclaiming your peace, and choosing to grow, even in the middle of the storm.

- RAW (Realize, Admit, Work through): Get real with yourself. Admit what's broken. Do the work to heal.

- RESET (Remember Every Situation Encourages Thought): Pause and think before reacting. Learn from what's happening instead of getting stuck in it.
- PATIENT (Pause And Think, Inhale/Exhale, Now Talk/Tap Out): Slow down your reactions. Respond instead of explode.
- FREE (Forgive, Release, Embrace, Elevate): Let go of what's holding you back. Forgive where you can. Step into who you're becoming.

Emotional Freeze

When you're so overwhelmed that you shut down, not because you don't care, but because you're just trying to survive. It's your mind's way of saying, "I need a timeout before I break."

Grieving the Living

The process of mourning someone who's still alive. Whether it's divorce, betrayal, or simply someone choosing to walk away, it's the kind of grief that hits different because they're not gone, but the version of them you loved is.

Reflection Prompts

1. What ACEs, if any, shaped the way you love or trust?

2. **What KHAOS skill do you need the most right now** RAW, RESET, PATIENT, or FREE?

3. What toxic loyalty have you held onto, and what would it look like to release it?

4. Which parts of your story are you ready to rewrite for yourself, not for anyone else?

References & Sources

Harvard Health Publishing. (2018). Understanding the stress response.

American Psychological Association. Understanding Anger.

National Institute of Mental Health (NIMH). Depression basics.

Kübler-Ross, E., & Kessler, D. (2005). On Grief and Grieving.

Van der Kolk, B. (2014). The Body Keeps the Score: Brain, Mind, and Body in the Healing of Trauma.

Brach, T. (2003). Radical Acceptance: Embracing Your Life With the Heart of a Buddha.

Centers for Disease Control and Prevention (CDC) & Kaiser Permanente. Adverse Childhood Experiences (ACE) Study.

Freyd, J. J. (1996). Betrayal Trauma: The Logic of Forgetting Childhood Abuse.

Journal of Family Psychology. (2020). Parental Grief and Child Outcomes.

Freud, S. (1920). Beyond the Pleasure Principle. (Repetition Compulsion)

Reader Reviews

"Because I didn't lose, I learned."

Get ready for the best rollercoaster ride you've ever been on.

It's up, down, twisted around. You'll find yourself screaming with your hands up, feeling anger with the author. You'll experience a numbness in your body after the drop, hands down, reflecting on the many emotional reactions that took place during the ride. Oh then there's the exhilarating part... the highlight at the end, the victory in finishing the ride.

Fighting through the fear, the highs, the lows, the twists and turns. And the realization that sometimes you even found yourself flipped upside down or going extremely fast in the wrong direction and calm after the storm of emotions. You get off the ride.

You're "excited" that you finally got a chance to say you did it... but you're not sure if you want to stand in line again for that ride for something to be over that fast.
(Forever never seems that long until you're grown)

It helps you understand that even when you were told something would last forever, it may not. Not because of fault, but lack of responsibility that's partially yours.

Grief explained so well. When you can see someone that has died in your mind.

OR like you wrote an obituary in memorance of someone you hear current stories about, still friends on social media and may even see at the cookout.

Whether it be a friendship, kinship or relationship, it's ok to let go and process the loss.

Based on experience, science and survival. An amazing read.
You can heal too…Let this book help guide you! – *K. Johnson*

"Through the lens of my lived experience and emotional truth."

Candice, reading your memoir was like breathing air I didn't know I
was gasping for. I felt seen. Affirmed. Like someone had finally
whispered the words I'd carried quietly for so long but never had the
space or language to release. You reached into the tender places, and
instead of flinching, you held them gently and honestly.

The part that broke me open—and stitched me back together—was
your exploration of detachment in the presence of deep longing. That
balancing act between craving emotional intimacy and knowing that
reaching for it in unsafe, unavailable places only deepens the wound.
You named the silence we sit in. You captured the ache in restraint.
And you made it clear: it's not weakness. It's wisdom.

Your words helped me disentangle love from longing, connection
from chaos. They reminded me that self-respect is quiet, unwavering,
and often painful in its clarity. That choosing peace—over being
chosen—requires a level of emotional maturity that doesn't come
easy but is deeply worth it.

You didn't just expose the pattern; you modeled how to break it. You
showed the beauty in staying present with discomfort instead of
numbing, how stillness can be a form of strength, and how walking
away from what diminishes you is not abandonment—it's liberation.

And if I may add what so few ever speak to: being a parent while
your heart is in a million pieces… I wouldn't wish it on my worst
enemy. The amount of tears you learn to hold back, the moments you
show up completely empty but still somehow pull from a source
beyond yourself, it's inexplicable. But you get it. On levels most
people can't imagine. Especially when the person who shattered you

136

remains tethered to your world because they are a "co-parent." There's no final goodbye. No clean break. Just constant reminders of what is and what will never be. That nuance alone made your words not just powerful—but sacred.

From my heart to yours, I'm forever grateful to know my opinion matters. Thank you for honoring not just your journey, but making space for the rest of us to examine ours. – *M. Ford*

"**Rating: 5/5**
Unflinching, therapeutic, and transformational. A must-read for anyone rebuilding after emotional devastation."

In *Grieving the Loss: How to Survive When the World Around You Dies*, Dr. Candice E. Cox delivers a soul-baring, psychologically grounded exploration of emotional devastation, personal betrayal, and the painstaking journey toward healing. This isn't just a memoir—it's a manual for anyone who's ever questioned their worth after loving someone who didn't know how to love them back.

At the center of the story is a gut-wrenching revelation: after 17 years of marriage and presumed monogamy, the author discovers she was unknowingly in an open relationship. The betrayal is staggering—not just from her partner, but from the narrative she had been living. Dr. Cox doesn't flinch. She dives straight into the rawest parts of her experience, shining a light on the often-unspoken truths about grief, shame, and the emotional casualties that accumulate silently over time.

What sets this book apart is its rare blend of emotional vulnerability and clinical insight. As a licensed therapist and trauma specialist, Dr. Cox navigates her personal journey through the lens of deep professional wisdom. Chapters like *"From CHAOS to KHAOS"* and *"FREE to Be"* are filled with tools that not only unpack trauma but offer readers a path through it. The "PATIENT" skill—Pause, And, Think, Inhale/Exhale, Now Talk/Tap out equips

137

readers with a simple, effective strategy for regulating their emotions and reclaiming their voice.

But perhaps the most striking power of this book lies in its truth-telling. Dr. Cox doesn't just recount what was done *to* her—she reflects on what she *allowed*, why she stayed, and the quiet, devastating ways we abandon ourselves in the name of love. It's a deeply courageous act to own both the heartbreak and the healing.

As she writes:

"We focus on what they did, but we rarely sit with what we allowed… the version of yourself you lost trying to keep them."

These words hit like a mirror. And that's what this book is—it's a mirror held up to all of us who have ignored red flags, swallowed our boundaries, or mistaken pain for purpose.

Grieving the Loss is not just about surviving betrayal—it's about confronting the silence that keeps us stuck, and finding the strength to rewrite our story. It's about grieving not just the person who left, but the parts of ourselves we lost trying to keep them.

Ultimately, Dr. Cox leaves readers with a message of reclamation, reminding us:

"You can love someone and still need to let them go.
You can forgive someone and still protect your peace."

This is a book for anyone who's been through the fire and is ready to stop merely surviving—and start healing on their own terms.

– S. Cooper

"I would suggest this book as a personal read but also a mental health resource."

In this book, Candice gives the reader a vulnerable view of what it is like to grapple with losing someone who is physically present. I enjoyed every moment of this book. The way she captures the reader with topics that every person can relate to makes the book even more desirable.

This is not just a read but also a work book. One has the chance to self-reflect on their own personal journey in healing of the topic. This makes the book even more personal. The questions use are thought-provoking, real, and forward thinking. It allows the reader to truly begin a healing process of their own. I would suggest this book as a personal read but also a mental health resource. I can see this book being used in therapy sessions and group discussions especially with the KHAOS skills she gives throughout the book.

As a therapist, I believe the first step to healing is through and this book is just that: a self-realization journaling piece that aides in personal growth. Get you a copy today! – M. Miller, MA, LPC

"A courageous, beautiful, relatable walk through healing after loss."

Candice provides a compassionate exploration and connection of divorce as not only a legal event, but a grief event.

You're walking through the endings of a marriage but also the endings of unhealthy attachments, themes, and reflections. All the while gathering tools on self- reflection, co-parenting, and rebuilding identity. It helps the reader to understand that healing is not linear. And healing after loss is possible.

A great guide to healing after loss. – *R. Shorter, LPC*

About the Author

Dr. Candice Cox, LCSW, is a trauma therapist, speaker, and the founder of **KHAOS Inc. (Keep Healing And Overcoming Struggles),** an internationally recognized framework that helps individuals and communities confront and heal from toxic and traumatic stress.

Rooted in both clinical training and lived experience, Dr. Cox blends raw truth with real tools to guide others through some of the hardest chapters of their lives. She has over 15 years of experience working with youth, families, and communities affected by generational trauma, violence, and emotional neglect.

Her work is deeply personal. As a survivor of both childhood and relationship trauma and a mother navigating co-parenting in the aftermath of divorce, she doesn't just talk about healing, she lives it.

Through her writing, speaking, and leadership, Dr. Cox continues to disrupt cycles of pain by giving people the language, the skills, and the unapologetic permission to heal out loud.

You can find her creating safe spaces, coaching individuals through the KHAOS Mindset, and reminding the world that healing is not a trend, it's a lifestyle.